STAR CHASER

STAR CHASER

Poetry by Mark Scheel
Photo Illustrations by Joseph Maino

Anamcara Press LLC
Lawrence, Kansas

Published in 2020 by Anamcara Press LLC
Author © 2020 Mark Scheel, https://www.pw.org/directory/writers/mark_scheel
Illustrations/Photography © 2020 Joseph Maino, www.JosephMainoPhoto.com
Book design by Maureen Carroll
Georgia, Timeburner, and Minion Pro.
Printed in the United States of America.

Book Description: A collection of poems that trace the arc of the life cycle—past, present and future—and reveal the heart of a poet.

ANAMCARA PRESS LLC
P.O. Box 442072, Lawrence, KS 66044
https://anamcara-press.com/

Ordering Information:
Quantity sales. Special discounts are available on quantity purchases by corporations, associations, and others. For details, contact the publisher at the address above.
Orders by U.S. trade bookstores and wholesalers. Please contact Ingram Distribution.

Publisher's Cataloging-in-Publication data
Scheel, Mark, Author
Star Chaser/ Mark Scheel

[1. POE023050   POETRY / Subjects & Themes / Family. 2. POE023030   POETRY / Subjects & Themes / Nature. 3. POE023040   POETRY / Subjects & Themes / Place.

ISBN-13: 978-1-941237-54-0 (Paperback)

ISBN-13: 978-1-941237-55-7 (Hardcover)

ISBN-13: 978-1-941237-56-4 (EBook)

Library of Congress Control Number: 2020936149

Old ghosts roam in and out my dreams,
And unpenned verse drifts blithely by.
Oh for the flame of a faithful muse
To coax them whole to the wakeful eye.

CONTENTS

YESTERDAY

TODAY

TOMORROW

ACKNOWLEDGEMENTS

A number of the poems in this collection were published in the following periodicals, blog series and anthologies as well as on two e-zines: *Autumn Harvest, Begin Again: 150 Kansas Poems, I-70 Review, Kansas Authors Club 2014 Yearbook, The Kansas City Star, Kansas City Voices, Kansas City Writers Group Holiday Collection–2007, Kansas Quarterly, The Midwest Quarterly, The New Times, The Pebble, Poemtrain.com, Potpourri, Pudding Magazine, Roguescholars.com, Show + Tell* and *Tallgrass Voices.*

The poem "Tethered Balloons" received first prize in the 2002 Basehor Community Library Poetry Month Contest. The poem "The Gardener" received honorable mention in the Cafe Poetica Winter 2002 Poetry Contest.

AUTHOR'S NOTE

Near the end of 1999 *The Kansas City Star* hired a new books editor who introduced a new feature in the Sunday Arts section—Poet's Corner—to showcase the work of area poets. My poetry writing had been on hiatus for a while, so I brushed up my skills and began submitting. Although week after week by-lines I recognized were appearing, nothing I sent in seemed to suit—even though several of my efforts were accepted for publication elsewhere. Whatever tack I took always met with failure at *The Star*, and as the months passed, the frustration and chagrin of this "*Star* chaser" only deepened. Although this new editor and I seemed to be on totally different artistic wave-lengths, I nevertheless vowed not to cease composing and sub-mitting until one of my creations graced the pages of *The Star*. Finally, on June 30, 2002—nearly two-and-a-half years after I'd tackled the challenge—a poem of mine did appear in Poet's Corner. But more important, by then, I discovered, I'd amassed nearly enough poems to constitute an entire book. It therefore seems only fitting that this collection of poetry be gratefully dedicated to the late John Mark Eberhart, former books editor of *The Kansas City Star*, and to his protracted and unremitting series of rejections without which many of the poems in this collection might never have been written.

M.S.

FOREWORD

In *Star Chaser*, Mark Scheel's newest poetry collection, we find the author transforming his grievances with contemporary, academically-inclined editorial tastes into a creative burst exploring the relationships among ancient legend, the life cycle, the autobiographical and modern day angst. Speaking as one myself who has encountered condescension toward poets not firmly ensconced in the university hierarchy, I appreciate the struggle to crack through the good-ol'-academe mentality and achieve publication in either literary or non-literary venues. As the new editor of *Poetry*, Christian Wiman, lamented in the January 2005 issue, "For poetry...to become professionalized is a disaster....The whole enterprise seems to have high walls around it." Thus, having formed a misfit poetic credo with Mr. Scheel and a band of like-minded poets and writers outside the existing perimeters of the established local "literati" by way of a group loosely known as the 5th Street Irregulars, I and Mr. Scheel have, like the goddess he alludes to in his book, made "a light of [our] own...."

Star Chaser is divided into three sections: "Yesterday," "Today" and "Tomorrow." This division, of course, signifies the reality all of us must confront living our lives. In the first section, the poem "Merging" might be seen as symbolizing conception as well as foreshadowing both young adulthood and growth. In "August Night" and several other poems we find the innate goodness and security of birth and childhood. One phrase, "As I grew greenly / into boyhood...," reminds me of the beautiful and yearning boyhood poems of Dylan Thomas and the vivid, nostalgic prose of Thomas Wolfe. In subsequent poems such as "The Colony Hotel That August," when he alludes to a steamy encounter with a waitress while "our beer cans / wept puddles," and the poem "Dandelion Sutra," we see the loss of childhood and innocence superseded by a dawning maturity and carnal knowledge. Finally, the poem "Witness" portends bare-boned, black-leather-jacketed visions of change and an uncertain future.

In the second section, "Today," we begin to see the initiation of another phase of life and a shifting of the zeitgeist. In the first poem, "Prairie Idyl," Scheel briefly alludes to the passing of his youth, the slow deterioration of rural America and the ultimate loss of his mother and a link to his own mortality. In the poem "This New Dawning," we begin to see a grim acceptance and a fear of the future after the shock of the events of 9/11. Another poem, "Coming Home from Iraq," is more stark and bleak as it envisions the implications of war, "the cold, polished marble of death." However, as all of us are coming to know, the world today is fraught with peril.

The third section, "Tomorrow," presents us with both a per-spective of looking back and looking ahead. Such bogeymen as retirement, aging, disease, terrorists and the great abyss of death all raise their frightening heads, yet there's also a counterbal-ance of hope for lasting love and internal peace. The speaker in the poem "The Gardener" has come to treasure the devotion he feels toward his wife far more than monetary gain. In "I Sleep with the Dead," the author recounts how even the simple event of going to sleep and awakening the next morning is something to be both philosophical and joyful about: "I bunk down at night / west-to-east, positioned as if / stretched out in my coffin." Yet even this seemingly final phase is tempered with an inherent sense of humor that belies the dark reality of looming doubts such as "more taxes and arthritis / and sin." But the last poem, "Tethered Balloons," best says it all when he physically and metaphorically releases the balloons and perhaps his own soul "into gospels of freedom" to "where tomorrow and yesterday / are one." And it should not go unmentioned that throughout the collection many of the poems are given an added richness and extended implication via the accomplished photography of Joseph Maino.

Such is the scope and beauty of *Star Chaser*. While Mr. Scheel may still deem himself poetically a "star chaser," it is clear that, like the Northern Lights themselves, he has illuminated our horizon with a book of poetry that transcends the emotionally empty and hollow halls of academe and reaches out, longingly and lovingly, to grasp and finally catch those faraway stars.

—Glen Enloe
author of *When Cowboys Rode Away*

THE LEGEND OF THE STAR CHASER

An ancient legend of unknown origin relates the chastening of the Goddess of the Clouds by the Supreme Lord of the Heavens. Since the beginning of eternity, the Cloud Goddess had possessed a great admiration for the dazzling light of the stars. She felt her own clouds deserved as much and thought them slighted at having been granted no light of their own.

On one particularly dark and overcast night, she crept up high into the heavens and snatched away the light from one unsuspecting little star. But, lo and behold, when she returned to her realm in the North, the light was so bright it set the whole north sky aglow. This situation did not go long unnoticed by the Supreme Lord of the Heavens, and he forthwith called the goddess before him to explain. To make matters worse, in the midst of the inquisition, the little darkened star appeared before them weeping over his lost light.

When all the facts were revealed, the Supreme Lord was furious and demanded the goddess return the little star's light with an accompanying profuse apology. And, as if that wasn't enough, the Supreme Lord imposed one further penance. Because of her proclivity toward envying the light, henceforth the goddess was condemned to chase behind shooting stars and comets, always burning in their trail but never possessing their light.

And so it was for many eons, until finally the Supreme Lord relented just a bit and decided to allow the Goddess of the

Clouds, for only a short time now and then, to possess a light of her own. And that's why, on occasion, one can observe in the heavens what has come to be known as the Northern Lights.

Now, it has been alleged by some that there are also certain human beings who are afflicted with the same longings as the Goddess of the Clouds. Human beings who yearn for the light of the stars and end up chasing in their trail. These humans, who chase after the stars, are called poets.

STAR CHASER

I
YESTERDAY

MERGING

It's always a dangerous maneuver—
zooming down off the Parkway
onto I-35 South,
the morning sun pink
in your eyeballs.
Two streams of purpose merging
by an instinct and bravado
fully understood by no one.

Split-second decisions at 60 mph,
all emotion compressed between
the brake and the accelerator,
one moment (for even the faintest
of heart) of living life on the edge.

Like the first time I reach out
to touch your hand,
the blood crashing inside my ears,
to draw you closer,
and closer still,
that first time,
knowing, all the while,
how we both
risk demolition.

CHRISTMAS MORNING

It wasn't the way the morning sun
        would paint the snow on the cedar
        windbreak pastel pink
        that draws this memory's heart
        home in December.

Nor the way the aroma of Mother's pastries
        baking in the kitchen
        and Grandmother's welcome laughter
        would wind throughout each room.

Nor even the way ancient, cherished decorations
        would revive their beauty upon the branches
        of some freshly anointed evergreen
        Father cut from the pasture.

Rather, it was that one Christmas morning
        seen through the eyes of a little boy.
        How he'd left a snack for Santa,
        and, upon waking, rushed barefoot
        in his pajamas to stare in awe.
        There was the half-eaten cookie
        Santa's fingers had held,
        the empty buttermilk glass
        his lips had touched —
        proof positive of his angel-like passage,
        the palpable sum of all goodness.

AUGUST NIGHT

The little Kansas farm with the creek
beside the corn rows and a pasture hill
above the red barn was for me
both womb and cradle. As I grew greenly
into boyhood, it traced endless paths
for my eager feet and paced the pulse
of my young heart. On August nights
when the day's heat held the darkness
breezeless and fireflies danced above
coyotes' howl and crickets' song,
my mother would leave my father's bed
to make a pallet on the living-room floor
by an open window facing north
to catch some air. I in my Roy Rogers
pajamas would steal in and nestle down beside
the silken curve of her warm body and
womanly fragrance. In those moments we were
like mare and foal together in straw.
Sometimes she would whisper to me,
laugh softly and touch my hair.
We'd listen as the train eight miles away
whistled, passing through the little
town of Allen, heading west toward California.
We had distant cousins in California who
sent us exotic gifts at Christmas, and I
dreamed of one day going there
to bring back palm trees and sea shells
to give my mother. I loved her like a goddess
and longed to grow up quickly and make her proud.
I'd lie awake in the summer stillness

beside her gentle, measured breathing,
and when I'd hear the train whistle, I'd make
a mighty wish that I could grow instantly to be
a giant like ones in stories she read to me.
If only I could burst out the window onto
moist, soft grass and stand taller than
our house and cedars in my bare feet.
Then I could step over the garden and vineyard
and hog-wire fence as I grew taller
and stronger with each pace.
I'd see the gravel road like a silver belt
beside me in moonlight and feel
wet slews and streams between my toes.
Faster I'd go, spanning pastures and hedges,
past windmills, haystacks and telephone lines,
until the shy, twinkling lights of Allen
lay before me and the searing locomotive's headlight
cutting the night. Then, as it passed the
blinking-red crossing, I'd leap astraddle its
thundering engine above the pumping round wheels.
I'd cry out, "All aboard!" My voice echoing
in the blackness from hills and valleys and
lonely farmsteads. Charging toward mountains
and desert and dream's end. Wind and smoke
racing through my hair. My arms spread wide
to gather in the stars.

THE COLONY HOTEL
THAT AUGUST

Mixing asphalt that summer to earn
college tuition, I met Dixie
in Paul's Café.

Her husband had pulled out for California.
She poured coffee like an angel,
had a room second floor, Colony Hotel.

In summer's heat, our lusty kisses
burst a flood across our souls
above the night stream that was Troost Avenue.

On the sill beside us our beer cans
wept puddles; the walls glowed
with neon fire.

I don't remember, when fall came,
what classes I attended, who taught them
or where they met.

But I never forgot the drag-queens'
banter, the sound of hookers' heels
on the stairs. How the nights burned
all that August.

Her sweet perfume
sweat into my hair.

A SON'S WAKE

For Roy

Mock orange memories and baby's-breath
to be—the arc of an arch
frames their anguish.

Tallow scent and tendered chant
can neither buffer nor balm
their hearts' needle.

The sun's cogwheel has fractured,
the Law of Gravity
gone upside down.

The celebrant worm rejoices in darkness—
a delicate fare
before its time.

A DAUGHTER'S GRADUATION

She can tell,
she knows,
how they must have
felt—Wilbur and Orville
that day at Kitty Hawk,
when after years
and years
of working
and wishing
and dreaming
and hoping,
they faced the sun
and the wind
and the rolling, green meadows
with the wheels turning
against the earth, faster
and faster,
then suddenly lifting,
free,
and they could fly!

Mark Scheel

THE LITTLE PINK HOUSE BELOW THE TRACKS

Emporia, Kansas, 1965

Under the reassurance of darkness,
since time immemorial,
the little pink house
below the tracks
stood watch as Black Mary
and her girls
entertained.
Railroaders
and college boys
jostled one another
traversing the narrow stone path.
And one night, as a Santa Fe brakeman
would tell it, a psychology student
on crutches and braces
hobbled in out of the snow.
He'd come, he announced,
for "behavioral research,"
and maneuvered over
beside the gas heater.
With all the maturity
his 19 years could muster,
he framed the central query:
"Tell me, Mary, just what was it
got you into this line of work?"

"Well, son," the old madam
 was said to reply,
"you see, it's kinda' like this.
 I put it out free
 for twenty years, and then
 I finally wised up!"

DANDELION SUTRA

*with apologies to Allen Ginsberg,
and Mahlon Coop*

I walked on the old Santa Fe railroad embankment in Emporia east of the weathered brick depot a block from Mary's pink cathouse and sat down under the shade of a diseased elm tree and a junked handcar to look at the sunset over Blaylock's Café and weep.

Mahlon Coop sat beside me on a protruding oily tie, a dissimilar soul, an undergraduate pup then, we had in common only an academic time and place (and the same girlfriend one weekend), digging our toes into the gravel ballast, thinking the same bleak thoughts of final week and our gut-rending squandered semester.

The stench of dead crawdads along the Cottonwood and Neosho commingled with the winds over IBP to waft putrefaction in our eyes and noses, as we pondered it all, our tongues parched from smoking dried corn silks, just ourselves like two spent hippies waiting for the crack of doom or the next lonely freight west.

Look at the Dandelion, Mahlon said, there was a dead gray shadow against the fill, big as a basketball, sitting dry on top of a huge cake of cow dung—

—I rushed down enthralled—it wasn't my first dandelion, but it was my biggest dandelion, memories of William Allen White— my kool-aid visions—the country school, my childhood visit to K.C.

and the Hells of the muddy Missouri and Wyandotte County,
    rusting bottle caps, crumbling pez dispensers, Marlboro butts and
    filters everywhere, ruptured diaphragms, the verse of the urban
    core, everything stained, the dank memory passing all gimcrack
    sharply into the past—
and the gray Dandelion poised in the sunset, flies circling its dung
base, dusty and speckled its urine-colored leaves, its stem Viagra
sturdy, the hoary flower ripe to loose its seed, the tiny hairs undu-
lating against the breeze like cobwebs,

serrated edges raised before the hostile march of railroad in one
    last defiant gesture, black coal particulate tracing its veins, its
    chlorophyll remnant sucking up the evening effluvia, a tumble-
    bug picking at its dung,
Unholy beaten-up old flora you were, my dandelion O my soul,
    I loved you then!
The grit was no student's grit but death and residue of iron handcars,
All that skirt and blouse of filth, that smoky insult to your face,
    that black industrial breath assaulting your sap, that hide of
    choked pollution stretched round your complexion—
And those dreary failing-grade fears and Denniston withered
    loveless nights, keen shards of broken Pepsi bottles, fish-stained
    pages of *The Emporia Gazette*, fungus-leaching sneaker soles, the
    ligaments of twisted Coors cans, the tendons of lost brassieres, the
    tongues of Prep-H caps, dear Lord what more could I name, every
    variety and variation of bestial sex organ and bodily sphincter—
    all these
Entangled in your dung-gorged roots—and you there waving
    before me in the sunset, all your glory in your conception!
A perfect beauty of a dandelion! a superb grand heavenly
    dandelion existence! a gentle round eye winking at the rising
    moon, alive and aroused and erotic and groping at the sunset
    shadows flaming evening breeze!
How many ants innocent of your taint tickled your petals while
    you cussed flower cusses at the Emporia hog-lot heavens?

Poor dying dandelion? when did you forget you were a
    dandelion? when did you look at your mottled crust and de-
    cide you were a barren filthy old handcar? the ghost of a hand-
    car? the wraith and spook of a once pumping up and down
    the tracks American handcar?
You were never no handcar, Dandelion, your were a dandelion!
And you Handcar, you are a junked handcar, forget me not!
So I reached down and plucked up the dandelion beauty from its
    manure foundation and thrust it heavenward like the Statue of
    Liberty torch, let the breezes burst its seed like a Fourth of July
    star shell, scattering dandelion legacy among the east Kansas
    clouds all the way to Johnson County,
and proceeded then to deliver my lecture to my own soul, and to
    Mahlon too now clapping his hands in cherubic joy, and to
    anyone else crazed enough to listen,
—We're not our skin of grime, we're not our pencils and note
    books, we're not our dirty underwear, we're not junked hand-
    cars rusting in the sunset, we're all beautiful golden dandelions
    inside, we're all rooted in rich brown Flint Hills dung, we're
    blessed by our genome and DNA and the hairy naked seed
    of our existence, and we are enjoined to spread our dandelion
    seed throughout the mad black streets and wanton prairies of
    our sit-down railroad handcar sunset Emporia elm tree Flint
    Hills academe hallucination.

THE SEASON OF BELIEVERS

> *"It is wrong always, everywhere, and*
> *for everyone, to believe anything upon*
> *insufficient evidence."*
> *~ W.K. Clifford*

Let me tell you a secret:
men and women alike,
at certain times, for recurring reasons,
(more than even securing salvation)
crave to be seduced.
Not, mind you,
by the purveyors of lust,
but rather by the dispensers
of faith. We are,
after all, the beneficiaries
of the gods and heroes
of Joseph Campbell. Whether from pulpit
or crystal ball, love letters
or hustings, how we do
relish good myth.
And if you question
how this can be so,
consider the following parable:

> *There was once, one mere lifetime ago*
> *a youth who went forth in*
> *the night streets of Fillmore*
> *in quest of magic dust*
> *for his sweetheart. The streets*
> *were dark and strange and lonely,*

and finally this youth met up
with a Johnny boy.* The Johnny boy's
suit looked oh so pretty; his gold
tooth gleamed when he smiled.
The Johnny boy inquired as to
the object of the youth's search
and immediately volunteered
his expertise.

He said he understood the need.
He said he had a sweetheart himself.
He said he had connections.
He said he'd be willing to help.
He said he could tell how they'd
          both had a hard life.
He said they were alike.
He said both of them deserved much better.
He said in truth he loved him like a brother.
He said if you can't trust your brother,
          who you gonna trust?
He said he'd take care of all the arrangements.
He said all he needed was the money.
He said, brother, all you gotta do is wait.

Thinking of his sweetheart
waiting in their love bed, the youth
entrusted his last ten dollars
to the Johnny boy.
Doffing his hat gaily, the Johnny boy
departed . . . never to be
seen again. And the youth waited.
And waited. Alone amid
the dark streets. Until
empty pockets and rage
devoured his effervescent faith.

But rage, unlike faith,
is a transient emotion.

Mark Scheel

Hence, the lessons of youth
are left behind with youth.
And so the first Tuesday in November
finds us all butt-deep in placards
bartering our hopes and dreams
with the Johnny boys.

O season of believers!
You beautiful dreamers!

W.K. Clifford must be
spinning in his grave.

✱The term "Johnny boy" is '60s slang denoting a street con man

CAPITAL GAINS

"And how did you fare
   during the former administration?"
   the young broker asked the pensioner.

"Well," answered the old man,
"it was like seeing a gold coin
   dropped down the pit of an outhouse.
   I rolled up my pant legs and sleeves
   and lowered myself down,
   and I came up with a coin.
   But it's gonna take me
   a month of Sundays
   to get the stink aired out."

SAMHAIN

Pumpkins by corn shock,
Straw-gold moon. Listen by door—
Small footsteps in night.

Tombstones cast shadows,
Owl calls in dark. Soul shivers—
Age-old lure of fright.

WITNESS

The splints, the blood-wet gauze
and stretcher gone.
The last remains, a fading siren's wail
and a witness—the biker—
numb-standing by the road.

He walks to his Harley-Davidson and mounts
deliberately. Pumps the starter
with a new respect,
looks both ways, and looks again.
Easy on the throttle. Acceleration measured.

He takes the by-pass west (he's traveled
this before), wide and straight
and traffic-free. The wind
is with him now below a sky
of turquoise hue, and as he rides
he feels again the steel
between his legs, the pleasing consort
of wheel and eye. He twists the
throttle tighter, cheeks relax.
Jacket leather cuts the air. Blacktop shoulder blurs
as on he speeds, hurtling down the road
he knows (the road he's
traveled many times before)—
secure, impregnable,
and blessed.

II
TODAY

PRAIRIE IDYL

Hail-stripped cottonwoods
weep like battered wives;
yesterday's wheat fields molder
in galvanized tombs.

It's been this way before:
the patriarchal sun turning
his gray side out like a banker
locking his door.

Main streets lie fallow
as desert bones. Tumbleweeds
dance on doorsteps.
Logo caps commiserate
round gun-racked pickup trucks
while only the crow's cry

mocks the stillness. And I—
turning a shoulder to the dark wind—
pilgrimage past the boarded school,
slip the wrought-iron portal's latch,
drop to one knee and lay a peony
on my mother's grave.

THIS NEW DAWNING

New York
September 2001

And what do we now know?

That "Godzilla movies" after all
possessed a dark, portentous truth?

That candlelight, acappella voices
and a breeze lofting the flag
can make you cry?

That wrestling ghosts
is awfully difficult work?

What I know is the firm skyline,
as viewed from my house deck,
is only a memory—
no, what I mean to say is,
the comfortable way I rested my hand
on the railing and contemplated the distance
is no more.

And no man knows what lies beyond.

BLOOD ANGER

And what does Muhammad caution?

That even when you think it's gone,
it's still there.
Like acrid smoke that lingers
above a razed temple,

the umbrage of a word or deed
clings on,
clouding the eye,
petrifying the heart,
converting muscle
to cold-quenched steel.

When morning breezes
brush eyelids open,
it's there waiting—
to suck the sugar from the dream,
to lurk like the shadow
of dark print
behind the page you're reading.

You may preach reconciliation,
wear the skin of magnanimity,
but a wrong remembered
can never be
a wrong forgiven.

Like a dried-blood stain
it's there forever,
a million tiny festers
suffused in every vein,
unrecanted and unresolved,

preserved till Judgment Day.

SEASON OF REVISION

Christmas 2001

This is our year-end of unease,
of colored lights on lamps of lonely hue,
of caroling voices with a tinge of ache
that turns the ear and hand
toward faint regret.

This is a season's closing without closure,
without tradition's zest for bow and bell,
without the leavened fullness of forgiving—
an overcast night
that chokes away the moon.

This is a time for retallies and revisions,
for distant ghosts behind the tinseled twigs,
for assessing and arranging what remains
to each and all of memory's
lore and legend.

This is a bloodletting of the heart
that seeks the petal pink of yesterday,
that beats and throbs itself against the grief
for what was loved,
and lost as to a thief.

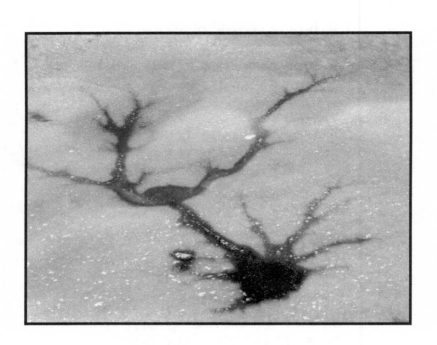

DARK ICE

Kansas City
January 2002

First ice on limbs, then metal jaws,
twisting, crushing, breaking;
what had once been
the nascent and hearty
trucked off to disposal.
No one green spring
can hope to redress
these stark, weeping scars.

How abruptly it descended—
this blue-black jolt from heaven—
force and counterforce
across our ordered arrangements,
stifling the givens,
leaving but a betrayal's memory
and the cold, dark distance
between us.

SOLDIER'S CHRISTMAS

On December 23—he remembers—
G2 detected a Viet Cong battalion
staging a night river crossing.
The 511th popped flares
and cut them to pieces
with M-60s, artillery and Cobras.
The next day they fished
black-clad bodies from sullied waters,
stretched them in rows.
It was the only way they had
to keep score.

The pall of their work
clung to them like smoke
in the vacuum of the Christmas Day
cease fire. Making their way
to the mess hall,
they sat down in rows
to canned turkey, cranberry juice
and Red Cross ditty bags
beside each plate. The chaplain
offered a prayer and then
led them in singing "Silent Night."
The words hung in their throats
like a bayonet's edge,
carving a moment's bridge
to that distant world
of red Santas, church candles
and hearth.

He sits today beside a festooned tree,
grandchildren laughing
among ribbons and wrappings,
their eyes like captured stars.
He listens as the anchor on CNN
drones of the Middle East and war
while young faces beneath helmets
drift across the screen.
He stares then past the tinseled twigs,
past the strung lights to distant shadows.
And there he sees the faces
and hears the rough carol
of the men of the 511th.
And he knows what all young soldiers
will learn—on the long road back
to the sanctity of home
the body count commingles with grace.

P.O.W.

The eyes always look the same—
Taliban, Iraqi, Viet Cong—
when the last chip's lost
and they come crawling out,
battered and filthy,
hands in the air,
bombs still ringing in their ears.
That deep-down, cowering shame
in the eyes—like a whipped dog
or a hungry child.

They had that look when
we flushed them from the tunnels
at Dac To and Xuan Loc.
The only difference now is distance—
viewing them on a screen
or below a headline
from the sanctuary of a recliner.

But there are those nights
when a cold north wind
touches the shrapnel
buried in your bones;
then when you lie down
and surrender to sleep,
you're back there again
in the steam and stench,
M-16 against your cheek,
cordite burning your nostrils,
those eyes pleading
with your trigger finger,
staring into your soul.

COMING HOME FROM IRAQ

Have you noticed, the way steel encases flesh,
body armor or casket—the same?

Coming back to the black hole in a city
where it all began.

Twelve thousand miles round-trip
to transport sand to the undertaker.

The moon sits behind the oak branch
like a spider peering down from a web.

Do you hear the cat pawing litter,
covering something up?

A night train clacks toward a crossing,
dissecting the heart with its whistle.

Tomorrow they will bend and touch
the cold, polished marble of death.

HOW TO FIGHT A WAR

The guns have fallen silent again."

"The last of the dead are laid to rest."
Victory is declared through a microphone.

"Our nation's flag has been furled."
"The troops are coming home once more."
The marching bands are poised and ready.

But what do you win when you win a war?
A scorched plot of ground to dedicate?
A song sung in your nation's name?
"Taps" played over a grave at sunset?

Maybe the illusion you can now shape history,
Turn a culture forward or backward.
Or make the wrong all right once more.
Or build new vistas with blackened ashes.
Send the devil back to his lair for a day!

On the debit side you've got some fixing to do:
Say some chosen words over the dead,
Reconstruct arms and legs that are missing,
Raise taxes again to pay for the cordite,
Write new speeches to reassure the bereft,
Flush nightmares out of heads that can't sleep.

Do you think down the road it balances out?
Tomorrow some diplomats will create new crises.
You'll have to pony up to upgrade your artillery.
Clear rubble to revive the villages you leveled
Because now your former enemy is your ally,

And your daughters have married his stalwart sons.
And you have all these treaties you must "honor."

Wars are fought by the young
Not simply because they're strong and able
But because they as yet have no memory.
The road laid with bricks of propaganda
With signposts pointing to glory and valor
Can seem as alluring to the callow eye
As a pusher pushing promises of white powder.
The "adventure" of a lifetime, you might say.

So, if offered a choice, what would I do differently?
For starters, only those men over seventy
Would be asked to answer the call to duty.
And only mothers above eighty would command them.
I'd put them on the line on a cold day in winter
When all they want is to drink hot coffee
And stand around toasting their backsides.
After a bit they'd be messaging the enemy
About whether their mittens and soup were warmer.

Or, "What are you using to tame your arthritis?"
After a while they'd call a truce,
Sit down together around a warm fire,
Open a bottle of wine and a photo album.
"Where are your grandchildren going to school?"
"Is this you dancing at your wedding?"
"How's your wife's health holding up?"
Finally, with a backslap, they'd call it a day,
Climb into a warm bunk—and go to sleep.
That is how I'd fight a war.

BEAR COUNTRY
Skagway, Alaska

The joystick has gone mushy;
the altimeter is in free fall.
Even a crash landing now,
in such bear wilderness,
seems beyond a prayer.

You concede gravity rules
when the dive becomes so grave
desperation supersedes complaint.
No more talk of parachutes or life rafts;
destiny now is hostage
to the bear's claw.

In these anguished moments
some will turn on one another,
accusatory and rending
like the bloody beast they fear—
all fang and fury and strained sinew;
only, in the end,
to cower like chastened children
awaiting their last comeuppance.

The joystick has gone mushy;
the altimeter is in free fall.
And the only question left is
how much longer
must we hold our breath.

But, while it lasted,
at the apex of our flight,
wasn't it a beautiful ride?
Dow: 7,590 Nasdaq: 1,228

45

Mark Scheel

PRICE CHOPPER AFTER MASS

She stops to decide
by the chili peppers,
Sunday lace bespeaking piety,
wafer and wine still fresh
on her lips.

Her children circle round
like small planets
orbiting their sun,
the tenor of her Spanish words
their gravitational pull.

Her husband, silent
beneath his Stetson,
stands watch with the cart;
his proud, brown muscles
are his statement.
He will pay from a wallet
secured by a silver chain.

The Germans would say:
"Kinder, Küche und Kirche."
The Latinos say simply, *familia*.

At the express check-out,
a fair-skinned girl
thrusts a hip
against her white shorts,
cradles her Virginia Slims
like gold.

Did she observe in passing
her dedicated sister,
gentle heiress of the Fifth Sun?

What warning
that sister conveys.

How much she herself has
to discover.

III
TOMORROW

SUNDAY SONATA

Near Gardez an al-Qaida fighter
chambers a brass round,
sights through evening's shadow.

Behind the stained glass of St. Pius
the mayor of Mission lies in state;
the priest, his gray beard mouthing
"body of Christ," tucks the Host
against a tongue.

On *This Week* file footage immortalizes
George Bush and Ted Kennedy
slapping each other on the back.

Across the living room a pensioner,
rising from his La-Z-Boy,
punches the remote power button off,
drops the Sunday edition
in the recycling bin.

As morning sun breaks onto
his dining-table top, he slides
the crystal center piece into its rays,
adjusts the polished planes
just so—and the walls
catch heaven's glow.

Like Midas his world is gold.

THE GARDENER

You've never possessed a green thumb
any more than a store of greenbacks.
Your wealth, it would seem, must lie
in some undetermined realm.
But sprouts and blooms are
her penchant. Her glory. She revels
in the seedling's promise,
the petal's delicate hue.
So each spring discovers both of you
haunting the gardening aisles at K-Mart,
perusing flower catalogues,
sharpening the shears and hoe.

"We'll put the marigolds
along the fence line," she says.
"The tomatoes in the corner,
the lilies under the oak."
And you concur dutifully
and begin to spade the loam.

But as you work, the rivulets of sweat
beckon ancient bonds.
You see, in the way her gloves flex,
your mother's hands at planting.
Her frayed straw hat is cousin to
those Granddad wore at harvest.
The set of her lips,
as she tucks in tender shoots,
was your late sister's look
skipping rope.

And then it's always the same.
On your knees beside the potting soil,
wiping the handkerchief across your brow,
poised in this seam of memory,
you think to yourself that you may be
the richest man alive.

SUMMER WALK

For Dee

The idle lane at dusk bends like a song
whose melody enfolds the fading light
so posing drowsy homes and oaks and hills
along the way in shadow. The summer balm

invites us toward sky's dying flare, our fingers
intertwine, words drift like dreams, our steps
the steps of children still discovering. How long
have we been thus? No less a generation

has been spawned beyond our door, cast its lot
and scattered—let it go! We have fretted
and toiled and failed and forgiven to stay the course
that brought us to this time and place and view.

Now we anticipate through evening's haze
the rusty reds and golds of autumn days.

ONE MOMENT IN TIME

"Time passing got here quick!"
My old high school chum speaks
through a hoary beard, crow's feet
deep beside eyes. He's referring
to an options trade.

We're walking through Loose Park,
a painter's palette of color
in crisp, fall air.
"It seems so," is all I respond,
rubbing my arthritic shoulder.

The dry leaves crunch
beneath our shoes—
echo of things past,
harbinger of what's to come.

FIRST FREEZE

Tonight marks season's
silent closure,
crystalline caution
on road ahead.

Pick the last tomato.
Cover the A/C.

What's left undone
is done.

I SLEEP WITH THE DEAD*

Astrologers, priests and necromancers
long ago decreed
the living shall sleep north-to-south
aligned in harmony with the poles.

The dead, on the other hand,
are laid to rest
parallel with the sun's path,
but west-to-east, so as
(at the appointed hour) to rise facing
the Second Coming.

The dimensions of the lake cabin
where I bait my fishhooks
preclude those hallowed traditions.
I bunk down at night
west-to-east, positioned as if
stretched out in my coffin.

And always I wonder —
as somnolence takes hold —
will my eyes open next
to a supernal choir, to cherubim
and a lighted path to glory?

Or — to the usual solar intrusion
beneath the window shade,
to more taxes and arthritis
and sin.

* The first poem that appeared in *The Star* Poets Corner.

Mark Scheel

TETHERED BALLOONS

How like we are—
afloat in lights and applause—
to tethered balloons
of delicate skin stretched taut
about empty space.
Tied to the illusion
of nights and days
by threads of grace,
we bob and waft
on an air
of roars and whimpers.
We trust our state
to be constant
as the clock's hands,
given like the moon and stars.
We take for granted tomorrow
as if time were stone,
only to rock in bewilderment
at the sudden gentleness
of severance—
at the sailing upward then,
above it all,
into gospels of freedom,
up and higher still to drift,
beyond the cool, soft grays
of eternity,
drawn, without provision,
to a boundless embrace
where tomorrow and yesterday
are one.

9 781941 237557